THROUGH
ARTISTS' EYES

The Living World

Jane Bingham

Raintree

www.raintreepublishers.co.uk
Visit our website to find out more information about **Raintree** books.

To order:
☎ Phone 44 (0) 1865 888113
🖹 Send a fax to 44 (0) 1865 314091
🖥 Visit the Raintree bookshop at **www.raintreepublishers.co.uk** to browse our catalogue and order online.

First published in Great Britain by Raintree,
Halley Court, Jordan Hill, Oxford OX2 8EJ,
part of Harcourt Education.

Raintree is a registered trademark of Harcourt Education Ltd.

Editorial: Isabel Thomas and Rosie Gordon
Design: Richard Parker & Tinstar Design www.tinstar.com
Picture Research: Hannah Taylor and Zoe Spilberg
Production: Duncan Gilbert

Originated by Chroma Graphics
Printed and bound in China by South China
Printing Company

10-digit ISBN 1 406 20152 9
13-digit ISBN 978 1 4062 0151 2

10 09 08 07 06
10 9 8 7 6 5 4 3 2 1

British Library Cataloguing in Publication Data

Bingham, Jane
   The living world. - (Through artists' eyes)
   1.Nature in art - Juvenile literature 2.Art - History - Juvenile literature
   I.Title
               704.9'43

Acknowledgements
The publishers would like to thank the following for permission to reproduce photographs: **p. 27**, © 1990, Photo Scala, Florence- courtesy of the Ministero Beni e Att. Culturali; **p. 35**, © 1990, Photo Scala, Florence/ Bayerische Staatsgemäldesammlungen, Neue Pinakothek Munich; **p. 8**, © 1990, Photo Scala, Florence/ Louvre; **p. 31**, © 1990, Photo Scala, Florence/ Louvre; **p. 28**, © 1990, Photo Scala, Florence/ Musee de Cluny; **p. 36**, © 1990, Photo Scala, Florence/ Musei Capitolini; **p. 24**, © 2003, Photo Scala, Florence/ HIP; **p. 12**, © 2004, Photo Scala, Florence/ HIP; **p. 45**, © ARS, NY and DACS, London 2006 Photo: © Art Resource, NY; **p. 41**, © Jeff Koons; **p. 47**, © Succession H. Matisse/ DACS 2006 Photo: Bridgeman Art Library/ Pushkin Museum, Moscow, Russia; **p. 43**, © Succession Picasso/ DACS 2006 Photo: © 1990, Photo Scala, Florence; **p. 23**, Alamy Images/ Michael Grant; **p. 18**, Ancient Art & Architecture Collection Ltd/ C.M. Dixon; **p. 13**, Ancient Egypt Picture Library/Robert Partridge; **pp. 7, 11** Axel Poignant Archive; **p. 30**, Bodleian Library, Oxford; Bridgeman Art Library pp. **33, 37; 9** (Ashmolean Museum, University of Oxford, UK), **15**, (Birmingham Museums and Art Gallery), **44**, (British Library, UK), **14**, (British Museum, London, UK), **49**, (Ca' Rezzonico, Museo del Settencento, Venice, Alinari), **17**, (Dinodia), **4**, (National Gallery, London, UK), **34**, (Private Collection), **40**, (Private Collection), **46**, (Private Collection, © Bonhams, London UK), **48** (Private Collection, Lauros/ Giraudon), **51**, (Private Collection, Roger Perrin), **39**, (Saarland Museum, Saarbrucken, Germany), **38**, (Stapleton Collection, UK); **p. 26**, E & E Picture Library/ Ken Murrell; **p. 5**, MirrorPix; **p. 29**, Science Photo Library/ Matt Johnston; **p. 20**, The Art Archive / Bodleian Library Oxford / The Bodleian Library; **p. 21**, Werner Forman Archive/ Museum of Anthropology, University of British Columbia, Vancouver; **p. 19**, Werner Forman Archive/ N.J.Saunders. **Cover**: *Elephant, Horse and Cow*, 1914 (oil on canvas), Marc, Franz (1880-1916) reproduced wih permission of Bridgeman Art Library/ Private Collection.

The publishers would like to thank Karen Hosack for her assistance in the preparation of this book.

Every effort has been made to contact copyright holders of any material reproduced in this book. Any omissions will be rectified in subsequent printings if notice is given to the publishers.

The paper used to print this book comes from sustainable resources.

Contents

Any words that appear in bold, **like this**, are explained in the glossary.

Introduction

A storm races through the forest, ruffling the grasses and leaves. There is a feeling of danger and excitement... and then you spot the tiger... Surprise!

The tiger is crouched ready to pounce. Its eyes are staring wildly and its fangs are bared. Even though you realize that this is not exactly how a real tiger looks, you still feel the power of the magnificent beast.

The French artist Henri Rousseau painted *Tiger in a Tropical Storm (Surprised!)* in 1891. It was the first of many images of animals in the jungle.

Rousseau was a self-taught artist who loved to visit the animals in the zoo. He also spent hours studying the tropical plants in the botanical gardens in Paris. All his paintings share the same sense of wonder at the mysterious world of animals and plants.

Henri Rousseau's tiger is not **realistic** in several ways. Its tail is too long and curly. Its eyes are too big and round, and its mouth is too red. But his picture helps us to imagine the secret world of the tiger. It also makes us think about the artist who painted it. Why did Rousseau choose to show the tiger the way he did? How did he feel about the tiger and what about the unseen creature that it is about to attack? (Rousseau later explained that the tiger was preparing to surprise a human explorer.)

Like many other images in this book, Henri Rousseau's painting aims to capture the spirit of the mysterious creatures that share our planet.

Henri Rousseau, *Tiger in a Tropical Storm (Surprised!)* (1891). This picture is painted in a childlike style, but it is still very powerful. What do you think it tells us about the artist's attitude to nature?

A range of art

This book covers a range of different **media**, including painting, **sculpture**, pottery, and **textiles**. It also includes examples of poetry and stories, photography, and film. Some of the works discussed here are by famous figures, such as Pablo Picasso, but many were produced by lesser-known artists.

The book starts by looking at **prehistoric** paintings of animals, and ends with a discussion of animal characters in films.

It explores art from all over the world. To help you see exactly where a work of art was made, there is a map of the world at the end of the book, on page 52. The timeline on page 53 provides an overview of the different periods of history discussed in the book.

For thousands of years, artists have created images of animals and plants. These images are very varied, but they all express their artist's delight at the living world around them.

Dancers perform a traditional Lion Dance to celebrate the Chinese New Year. Their colourful costume doesn't look at all like a real lion, but the Lion Dance is still a powerful expression of the lion's wild spirit.

The hunted and the hunters

As soon as people started painting pictures, they showed animals. Paintings have been found in caves in southern France that date from around 30,000 years ago. These prehistoric pictures were painted by hunters. They show bison, deer, and wild horses.

Prehistoric animals

Animals in prehistoric paintings are simple in form, but confidently drawn. The animals are usually shown running, and seem full of life and energy. Prehistoric artists used a wide range of colours made from natural **pigments** including red, yellow, orange, brown, and cream. They blended these colours together very skilfully, and shaded parts of the animals' bodies so that they looked solid and real. It is clear that the early cave painters watched the creatures they painted very closely and often studied them in action.

Nobody knows exactly why the early artists made these animal paintings. The paintings may have been used as teaching aids to instruct young hunters. They may also have had a religious or magical meaning. Animal paintings in caves were probably associated with special ceremonies held before a hunt.

Animals in North Africa

Thousands of years ago, the Sahara desert in North Africa was not a desert area.

The people who lived there hunted elephants, rhinos, ostriches, and giraffes and they painted pictures of these animals on rocks. These early animal paintings date from 20,000 years ago.

Around 2000 BCE, the land in North Africa started to dry up, and the people were forced to stop being hunters. They became cattle herders instead, and their artists began to paint pictures of cattle.

San paintings and dances

Some traditional people in Africa still paint images of animals on rocks. The San people of Southern Africa have been painting **elands** (a type of antelope), for thousands of years. They have a special antelope dance associated with their paintings of elands. San artists say that when they paint an eland, they somehow manage to gain some of the animal's grace and power.

Natural pigments

The San people of Southern Africa use a range of natural pigments in their paintings. Red ochre is made from ground-up rock. White is made from a type of clay, and black is produced from **charcoal** or soot. The pigments are ground into a fine powder and mixed with a binder, such as blood or egg white, which holds the mixture together.

This Aboriginal image of a crocodile was painted on a rock in Arnhem Land, in northern Australia. Like the San people in Africa, the **Aboriginal people** of Australia have continued the ancient tradition of painting animals on rocks. The oldest rock paintings found in Australia date from around 20,000 BCE.

Ancient hunts

In many ancient civilizations, hunting was part of everyday life. Poor people hunted animals for food, while rulers went out hunting for sport. Meanwhile, painters and carvers produced accurate images of the creatures being hunted. They also showed the animals, such as dogs and horses, that helped the hunters to pursue their prey.

Carvings and paintings from Ancient Egypt show **pharaohs** in their chariots, chasing after gazelle, antelopes, and ostriches. Sometimes artists also show sleek hunting dogs running beside the pharaohs' chariots. A few Egyptian carvings show hippo hunts. Hunters stand in their boats and throw spears at the hippos, who thrash around in the water, with spears sticking out of their bodies.

A carving from the kingdom of Assyria (present-day Syria) shows the king hunting lions in his royal hunting park. These carved lions are magnificent-looking beasts with shaggy manes and powerful limbs. Lion hunts also took place in Ancient Greece. A tomb from Ancient Greece shows the hero Alexander the Great fighting a massive lion, armed only with a shield and spear. All these early images emphasize the power and size of the wild creatures being hunted.

This detail from an Assyrian carving shows King Ashurbanipal setting off on a lion hunt. The carving includes dramatic images of lions and horses in action.

Medieval hunts

Hunting was a favourite sport of **medieval** nobles and kings. They raced through the countryside on fast horses, following packs of hounds. Hunters chased after wild bears, deer, boars, foxes, and hares – all common animals in medieval Europe.

The hunt was a very popular subject in medieval art. Artists often painted pictures of hunts in **manuscripts**, and **tapestries** of hunts were hung on castle walls.

Medieval pictures of hunts are usually very lively. They often feature leaping deer, galloping horses, and racing dogs. The images **portray** a sense of the grace and speed of all these animals. In particular, they show the stag as a noble and mysterious creature.

Tapestries of hunts sometimes covered several walls. They show the main events of the hunt but also include the trees and flowers of the forest. Many hunting tapestries feature small creatures, such as squirrels, rabbits, and birds. These early images of woodland life are very detailed and carefully observed.

The hunter or the hunted?

A scene from the margins of the Ormesby **Psalter**, a 14th-century prayer book, shows a hunting scene with a difference. Here, a giant rabbit holds a bow and arrow, and aims at a huntsman who is running away as fast as he can. In this comic scene, the artist reverses the roles of the hunter and the hunted. Medieval artists liked to give human roles to animals. They sometimes showed a fox preaching in a church and a monkey acting as doctor.

Paolo Uccello, *Hunt in the Forest* (c. 1470). Uccello's famous painting features lively but stylized horses, hounds and deer.

Powerful protectors

Different people around the world feel very close to certain animals. They often see these creatures as powerful protectors. Some people also believe that they are descended from animals.

Animal ancestors

The Aboriginal people of Australia believe that powerful **Ancestor** Spirits created their land and everything in it. These spirits mainly took the form of animals, such as snakes, turtles, or birds. Throughout the Aboriginals' long history, their artists have produced images of the Ancestor Spirits, and Aboriginal artists today still paint pictures of their animal ancestors.

The Rainbow Serpent

One of the most powerful Ancestor Spirits is the Rainbow Serpent, a colourful, giant snake. The image of the Rainbow Serpent often appears in traditional **bark paintings**, but it is also shown in modern canvas paintings. Aboriginal artists usually show the Rainbow Serpent with a fierce, biting head and a long, gliding body, covered with patterns. In some paintings, the Rainbow Serpent is shown giving birth to the first people. Inside the serpent's body are tiny figures of men, waiting to be born.

African animal masks

In traditional African societies, people often create masks like animal heads.

They wear these masks for dances during ceremonies where they ask the animal spirits for help. The Dogon people of West Africa rely on the spirit of the antelope to help them in their daily farming work. They create rectangular antelope masks with several horns sticking out of the top. Dancers wearing the masks hit the ground with sticks. This represents the movement of an antelope pawing the ground with its hooves.

In other parts of Africa, people make a range of animal masks. The Nuna people of Burkina Faso carve masks in the shape of crocodiles, buffaloes, and hawks and call on these powerful animal spirits to keep them safe from danger. Wooden Nuna hawk masks have a carved bird's head with large staring eyes and a snout-like beak. This fierce hawk's head is flanked on either side by wide outstretched wings.

Patterns with meanings

The Nuna hawk mask is decorated with patterns that have special meanings to the Nuna people. For example, the zigzag lines on the hawk's wings represent the difficult path that their ancestors had to take through life. The chequer-board pattern of black and white shows the contrast between night and day.

In many Aboriginal paintings, animals have a magical meaning. This bark painting was created in honour of the Rainbow Serpent Spirit Ancestor. It shows four serpents wound around a man with his animals and plants. The serpents appear to be protecting the man.

Animal guardians

From the time of the earliest civilizations, artists have carved images of fierce animals. People believed that these frightening creatures could act as guardians, and protect them. These animal guardians were placed in important positions, such as doorways. They were meant to make their people feel safe and to frighten away any enemies. Some of the guardians were modelled on real animals, such as lions or bulls. Others combined the features of several different animals.

Ancient guards

Around the year 575 BCE, the people of the ancient city of Babylon built a massive gate leading to their city. They covered this gate with a series of giant figures of bulls and dragons. These magnificent creatures are made from thousands of tiny pieces of **mosaic**. They are coloured gold and brown and stand out proudly against their turquoise background. The bulls look strong and powerful, while the dragons seem magical and mysterious. Together, they send out the message that any enemies would be best to keep away from the city.

The splendid palace of Nimrud, in Ancient Assyria, was built around 850 BCE. At the heart of the palace was the royal throne room, protected by a pair of massive stone creatures. These creatures had the powerful combination of the head of a man, the wings of an eagle, and the body of a lion.

The restored entrance gate to the city of Babylon. For visitors, these larger-than-life guardian animals would have been a magnificent sight.

Egyptian animal gods

The Ancient Egyptians worshipped many gods and goddesses, and several of these gods had the heads of animals or birds. Horus, the god of the sky, is shown in paintings and carvings with a falcon's head. Anubis, the god of death, has the head of a jackal, and Amun, the creator, has a ram's head. The goddess Taweret took the form of a hippo. She looked after pregnant women and babies.

The goddess Bastet was the protector of cats. She is sometimes shown as a woman with a cat's head, and sometimes represented simply as a cat. One surviving **sculpture** shows the goddess as a slim and elegant, pointed-faced cat.

Egyptian cats

The Egyptians had a great respect for cats because the cats protected their precious grain from mice. Many people kept cats as pets, and anyone who killed a cat could be put to death. When a family cat died, the family mourned for it, shaving off their eyebrows to show their sadness. When the cat of a pharaoh died, its body was preserved as a **mummy**.

An Ancient Egyptian carving of the god Anubis, with a jackal's head. Jackals feed on the bodies of dead animals, and Anubis was the god of the dead.

Jaguars of the Maya

The warlike Maya people lived in Central America between 300 BCE and 1500 CE. They built stone cities deep in the rainforests and carved massive stone heads to protect their cities. The heads had wide-open jaws filled with vicious-looking, pointed teeth. These fearsome guardians were clearly based on the jaguars that prowled the surrounding forests.

Aztec creatures

The Aztec people settled in central Mexico around the year 1300 CE. They were skilled craft workers, who created ornaments from **semi-precious stones** such as turquoise. One surviving ornament shows a serpent with a wavy, snake-like body, and two savage biting heads. The Aztec people believed that snakes had special powers.

They worshipped several serpent (snake) gods, including Quetzalcoatl (the feathered serpent), Xiuhcoatl (the fire serpent), and Mixcoatl (the cloud serpent).

The Aztecs made colourful folded books, known as **codices**. These contain many images of animals, including birds, snakes, and jaguars. The codices also show Aztec **knights** dressed in animal costumes. Eagle knights wore a suit of feathers, with eagle's talons covering their feet, a long feathery tail, and a helmet made from an eagle's head and beak. Jaguar knights dressed in a jaguar's skin, with their head emerging from the jaguar's jaws. Aztec warriors believed that when they dressed as eagles or jaguars, they took on some of the qualities of those animals, becoming swift and fearless.

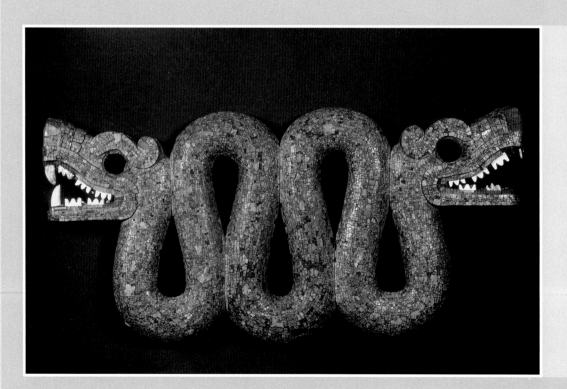

An Aztec serpent brooch, made from turquoise and other semi-precious stones. The Aztecs believed that serpents had special powers. So, a brooch like this could protect its wearer from harm.

The Nazca people were famous for their animal whistling jars. This jar is decorated with a painting of a condor (a kind of vulture). The image of the condor looks remarkably modern, even though it was painted almost a thousand years ago.

Animal warriors

The Aztecs were not the only warriors to wear animal costumes. On the central plains of North America, Native American chiefs dressed in buffalo skins and wore headdresses made from eagles' feathers. As well as wearing costumes that linked them to animals, Native Americans often gave themselves animal names. So, a chief might be named Sitting Bull or Running Deer. Names like these showed the Native American people's respect for the animals all around them.

Nazca jars

The Nazca people lived in South America from around 200 BCE to 600 CE. They produced pottery jars in the shape of creatures, such as fish, ducks, and turtles. Some of the jars had spouts and mouthpieces and could be blown as whistles. **Archaeologists** think that these whistling jars were used in religious ceremonies in which the Nazca people made contact with powerful animal spirits. Priests may have blown into the whistling jars to give the animal spirits a voice.

Animals of India

In the 6th century CE, people in India began to carve massive temples from rock. These mountain-shaped temples were covered with carvings of **Hindu** gods and goddesses. Many of these carved gods take the form of different creatures, and some of the gods ride on animals, such as a bull or a rat. These religious creatures have many meanings, but the Hindu artists clearly observed the animals and birds of India when they were carving and painting them.

Ganesha and Hanuman

One of the best-known Hindu gods is Ganesha, the god of wisdom and learning. He is shown with an elephant head, four arms, and two legs. Carvings of Ganesha often show the god with a round belly and a jolly, smiling face. Sometimes Ganesha is even shown dancing, with his trunk and his arms waving in the air. Although Ganesha does not strictly resemble an elephant, it is clear that the Indian **sculptors** were familiar with real elephants and their playful behaviour.

Another common figure in Hindu art is Hanuman, the monkey god. Statues of Hanuman are often placed as guardian figures outside a temple. Hanuman is frequently shown as a lively, mischievous god.

The incarnations of Vishnu

Hindus teach that their god Vishnu has had nine different lives, or **incarnations**. In several of these incarnations he took the form of an animal. Vishnu is shown in carvings and paintings as a fish, a turtle, and a boar — all animals that are found in the Indian countryside.

Rats and bulls

Several Hindu gods are shown riding on an animal's back. For example, the god Shiva rides a bull, called Nandi, while Ganesha is sometimes carried by a very strong rat. Most carved scenes featuring Ganesha also include his helpful rat, hidden somewhere in the picture.

Nandi, the bull who carries Shiva, is a very important figure for Hindus. All over India, sculptors have created statues of Nandi. The bull is a **sacred** animal in the Hindu religion. Hindus are not allowed to harm bulls or cows, or to eat their meat.

An Indian painting showing Ganesh, the elephant god. Ganesh sits in a chariot that is pulled by five rats. Images of Ganesh and his rats vary greatly. In some paintings, they look quite realistic.

Beasts of the sea

Some early seafaring people carved images of ferocious creatures on the **prows** of their fighting ships. They believed that these creatures would terrify their enemies, and also help to guide them safely through the seas.

Ancient Egyptian warships had pointed wooden prows for ramming the sides of enemy ships. At the end of each prow was a golden lion's head. The lion heads gave the ram extra strength, but also presented a frightening sight as they headed towards the enemy ships.

The Ancient Greeks decorated their warships by painting a large staring eye on either side of the prow. They also fixed a single horn, like a rhinoceros' tusk, between the painted eyes. The horn served a double purpose. It frightened off enemy ships and made sure that they didn't approach too close. The Greeks believed that the painted eyes helped the ship to find its way safely through danger. Even today, many Greek sailing boats still have eyes painted on their prows.

At the end of the 8th century CE, Viking raiders from present-day Scandinavia began to launch attacks on the shores of Europe. They crossed the sea in long, narrow warships with tall wooden prows. At the end of each ship's prow was a carved animal head. Viking prows showed wild-looking creatures, which were half dragon and half eagle, with cruel,

curved beaks, and staring eyes. The sight of these fearsome creatures riding the waves towards them must have terrified the people on the shore.

Celtic patterns are often filled with strange creatures. Here, you can see six dragon heads and two bird-like creatures.

Celtic beasts

The Celts lived in northern Europe during the **Middle Ages**. They were famous for their fierceness in battle and for their finely carved swords and shields. Celtic weapons are covered in carvings of wild beasts. The beasts take the form of serpents with fierce, biting heads, winding around each other to form swirling patterns. Celtic warriors believed that these magical beasts gave them extra protection in battle.

Patterns made from biting beasts were not just used for weapons. They are also found in Celtic jewellery, stone carving, and manuscripts.

Totem poles

The heads of fierce beasts feature in the art of some Native American **clans**. The people of the northwest carve and paint fierce animals on **totem poles**. The carvings are based on the animals of the northwest, and include grizzly bears, killer whales, and wolves.

A Native American totem pole, carved and painted with a traditional design.

Mythical creatures

Some of the creatures shown in ancient and traditional art are not real animals at all. Instead they are **mythical** beasts with special, magic powers. Often, very similar mythical creatures appear in the art of many different cultures.

The phoenix and the firebird

In many parts of the world, people tell stories about a "firebird". One of the earliest surviving firebird legends comes from Ancient Egypt. Here, the bird is shown as a golden phoenix (a bird very similar to an eagle) and it is usually pictured rising from a fire. According to Egyptian legend, the phoenix lives for 500 years. Then it is destroyed in a fire and reborn from the ashes, beginning a new cycle of life. The Ancient Egyptians and the Ancient Greeks used the phoenix as a symbol of new life.

This **medieval** painting shows a phoenix rising from the flames to begin its new life. It comes from a 12th century **bestiary**. Bestiaries contained pictures and information about animals, both real creatures and mythical beasts.

20

The legend of the firebird flourished in ancient China, where it was known as "Feng-huang". This miraculous bird was a popular subject for artists in the past, and it is still shown in Chinese art today. In some areas of China, artists show Feng-huang with a large bill, a snake's neck, the back of a tortoise, and the tail of a fish. Other artists paint images of a brilliant scarlet bird with the head of a pheasant and the tail of a peacock.

In Hindu art the firebird is "Garuda", who pulls the chariot of the Sun. Garuda is usually shown with the beak, wings, talons, and tail of an eagle, and the body and legs of a man.

The firebird also appears in Russian folktales and traditional art. Known as "Zshar-ptitsa", it is a magical bird that lights up the dark and heals the sick with its chants. Zshar-ptitsa is shown in traditional Russian paintings with silver and gold feathers, dropping pearls from its beak as it sings. In 1910, the Russian composer Igor Stravinsky turned the legend of Zshar-ptitsa into a famous ballet called *The Firebird*.

Images of the Thunderbird

Many Native American tribes have a legend of the Thunderbird. According to traditional beliefs, this giant creature is responsible for thunderstorms. When it beats its massive wings it makes thunder.

It shoots lightning from its golden beak. Images of the Thunderbird have been found in carvings and paintings from the Pacific Northwest, the central Plains, and the Northeast of America. Sometimes the Thunderbird resembles an eagle and sometimes it looks like a snowy owl.

This carved Thunderbird mask comes from the northwest coast of America. It was used in sacred dances performed by the Kwakiuti people.

Mixed-up creatures

Many creatures in ancient and traditional art are made up of two or more animals. For example, the griffin, which appears in the art of Ancient Mesopotamia and Ancient Egypt, has the head of an eagle and the body of a lion. The sphinx and the mermaid are also combinations of different creatures. The sphinx has the head of a human and the body of a lion, and the mermaid has a woman's head and body, with a fish's tail.

Beasts and bestiaries

The people of the Middle Ages were fascinated by strange creatures. Scholars collected all the information that was known about unusual creatures and put it all together in illustrated manuscripts known as bestiaries. Some of this information came from observing real animals, but most of it came from myth. Medieval bestiaries include real animals, such as cows, elephants, and whales. Bestiaries also contain mythical beasts, such as the griffin and the unicorn.

The animals in the bestiaries were often used to teach people lessons. The lion was an example of bravery and strength, while ants and bees showed people how to lead a hard-working, useful life.

Unicorns

The snowy-white unicorn, with a single horn rising from its head, appears in medieval carvings, paintings, and tapestries.

It was seen as a symbol of perfect purity. The unicorn is the subject of a famous tapestry, known as *The Lady and the Unicorn*, which was made in Flanders (present-day Belgium) around 1500. This tapestry tells the story of how a pure maiden captures a unicorn. Unicorns are usually impossible to catch, but the maiden holds up a mirror to the magical creature. The unicorn approaches and looks at its own image in a mirror. Then it gently lays its head in the maiden's lap.

Unicorns still capture the imagination of artists and storytellers today. Even cartoon films have been made about them. The unicorn also appears in coats-of-arms. The British royal family's **coat-of-arms** is supported by a lion and a unicorn.

Animals in the stars

Around 3,000 years ago, the Ancient Greeks looked at the shapes made by certain groups of stars, and saw the outlines of animals. They gave the names of animals to these groups of stars, or **constellations**, and told legends about them. Animal constellations include Aries the ram, Cancer the crab, and Taurus the bull. Artists have shown these creatures in their carvings and paintings for thousands of years.

The unicorn is a symbol of goodness and purity. This carved unicorn originally stood guard over the entrance gate to London's central law courts.

A medieval painting showing Saint George fighting a dragon. According to legend, Saint George had to kill the dragon in order to rescue a princess (seen on the left). In the Middle Ages, dragons were associated with wickedness. When George kills the dragon it is a victory of good over evil.

Monsters and dragons

Monsters and dragons feature in the art of many cultures. They represent the forces of danger in the world. These monsters are often based on real animals, such as lizards and snakes, but artists try to make them look as frightening as possible.

Medieval dragons

In the Middle Ages, painters and sculptors showed Saint Michael and Saint George fighting bravely with fire-breathing dragons. Medieval dragons usually look like giant lizards, with green, scaly bodies. They also have snapping jaws and bat-like wings.

Dragons don't just feature in the religious art of the Middle Ages. They also appear in folk art, poems, and stories, attacking brave heroes or guarding heaps of treasure. In the poem *Beowulf*, written around 700 CE, the hero has to fight against two water monsters and a dragon.

Chinese dragons

In Ancient China, the dragon was worshipped as a powerful god. Even today, dragons are often shown in Chinese art. Dragons are painted on **porcelain**, and carved in **jade** and bronze. Images of dragons are also carved on the roofs of temples to frighten away any evil spirits that might try to enter the building.

The early Chinese emperors wore magnificent robes, embroidered with dragons. The dragons had massive swirling tails, open jaws filled with teeth, and long, sharp claws. In Ancient China, only the emperor was allowed to wear a robe embroidered with dragons. When he was dressed in his dragon robe, the emperor gave out a powerful message of power and strength.

Dragon dancers

The dragon dance is an important festival in China. In Ancient China, people performed a special dance to please the Chinese dragon god at springtime. Nowadays, the dragon dance is still performed every spring. People make models of a dragon's head and body, using bamboo, wood, cloth, and paper. Then they fix the models to poles that are held by a column of dancers. A dragon can be up to 100 metres (330 feet) long. During the dance, the dancers all move together, leaping and crouching to the beat of a drum. A skilful team of dancers can make the dragon form special patterns. These patterns have names such as "going around the pillar" and "cloud cave".

Plants, flowers, and fruit

For thousands of years, artists and craft workers have been inspired by plants, fruits, and flowers. Some artists have produced detailed, realistic images. Others have used the shapes and colours of plants as a starting point for patterns and designs.

Carvings from plants

In Ancient Egypt, **sculptors** carved borders for their buildings. These borders were based on a palm leaf design. Later, Greek sculptors used the stiffly curving forms of the **acanthus** plant in their buildings. The Greeks invented a column, with a design of acanthus leaves at its top, which became known as the "Corinthian column". This style of column was used in Greek and Roman buildings.

The sculptors and woodcarvers of medieval Europe filled their cathedrals and churches with carvings. These carvings often featured common plants and fruits, arranged in attractive shapes. Oak leaves and acorns, hawthorn leaves, and vine leaves were especially popular. Sometimes carvers showed birds, mice, or squirrels peeping out of the leaves.

The "Green Man" was a popular subject for medieval carvers. He was a wild nature spirit who was believed to live in the woods. Carvers showed the Green Man's head surrounded by leaves. Some carvings even show him with leaves growing out of his face.

In the 17th century, carved wooden furniture became very popular in English country houses and cathedrals. One outstanding master of this art was the Dutch woodcarver Grinling Gibbons. He produced exquisite oak and limewood carvings featuring birds, flowers, and fruit, all carefully observed from nature.

A restored medieval stone carving of the Green Man. In the Middle Ages, some people believed that the Green Man lived in the woods. He was seen as a spirit of nature.

Manuscripts and windows

During the Middle Ages, skilled artists created hand-written books known as manuscripts. These artists, who were usually monks, copied out texts by hand and decorated them in glowing colours. The margins of the manuscripts were often filled with delicate, swirling, and branching designs, based on plants and flowers.

The trailing, twirling plant patterns found in manuscripts were also used in some medieval windows. These windows were filled with plain glass, **etched** with delicate patterns of plants and leaves. This type of decorated medieval glass is known as *"grisaille"*.

A carved wooden panel by Grinling Gibbons, featuring birds, fruit, and flowers. The panel shows Gibbons' incredible skill, and his careful observation of nature.

27

Thousands of flowers

By the 15th century, artists were very skilful at showing flowers. Even weavers of tapestries were producing remarkably detailed images of plants. Medieval tapestries included hundreds of different herbs and flowers in their backgrounds. The patterns created by these plants and flowers are known as "*mille fleurs*", which is French for "thousands of flowers".

Studying plants

Some medieval monks grew herbs in special gardens, and turned these herbs into medicines. They studied the plants carefully, making detailed drawings, describing their flowers and fruit, and noting what medicines could be made from them. These careful observations were made into reference books, known as herbals.

In the 15th and 16th centuries, two outstanding artists took the study of plants onto a new level. The surviving sketchbooks of the Italian Leonardo da Vinci and the German Albrecht Dürer reveal that both these famous artists made incredibly detailed drawings of plants. They also included realistic flowers and plants in their paintings.

The Lady and the Unicorn tapestries were made around 1500. These six tapestries contain hundreds of different flowers and herbs, and all of them can be identified as real plants. The tapestries also contain many small animals and birds. How many creatures can you find here?

Botanical studies

From the 16th century onwards, people began to study plants very carefully. This was the beginning of the science of **botany**. Many botanists were also skilled artists who created detailed drawings, recording each stage of a plant's life cycle. These beautiful drawings were usually drawn in pen and coloured with inks mixed with water. The drawings were reproduced as coloured prints and published in volumes of botanical studies.

Interest in botany increased sharply as people began to explore different parts of the world, and botanists recorded the exotic plants they discovered. In particular, the paintings of Australian plants made by the artists who sailed with Captain Cook became very famous.

By the 18th century, artists were creating images of flowers that were works of art in their own right. One of the most famous botanical illustrators was the French royal flower painter Pierre-Joseph Redouté. During his career, Redouté produced over 2,000 detailed flower studies.

Flower photography

In the 20th century, botanical drawing was gradually overtaken by photography. Today, some photographers produce amazing close-up images of flowers using high-resolution digital cameras. Because we are not used to seeing flowers so close-up, they can look like **abstract** paintings. Other artists use speeded-up film to show flowers growing, and producing buds and flowers.

A close-up photograph of a begonia. Startling images like this can look more like paintings than photos. Notice the tiny fly on the flower's petal!

Tricking the eye

One late medieval manuscript contains some remarkable images of flowers. *The Book of Hours of Mary of Burgundy* is a personal prayer book, produced for the Duchess of Burgundy in central France. It contains a series of painted religious scenes, but its most remarkable features are the paintings in the margins. Here, the **anonymous** 15th-century artist has painted flowers in such a realistic way that they seem to be real flowers laid on the page. On some pages, the artist even shows a butterfly perching on the flowers, as though it has just landed on the book. These very skilful nature studies are known as "*trompe l'oeil*" images, which is French for "trick the eye". In the following centuries, many painters of flowers worked in the *trompe l'oeil* tradition.

Still life

During the 17th century, a new type of painting began in Holland. It was known as **still life**. Dutch artists such as Balthasar van der Ast, Adriaen von Utrecht, and Jan van Huysum painted glowing pictures, showing careful arrangements of fruit and flowers.

The Dutch masters worked with oil paints and very fine brushes to show fruit and flowers in astonishing detail. They even showed tiny veins in the flowers' leaves, and petals stained with pollen. However, not all the details in a Dutch still life were based exactly on what the artist saw.

Often, the artists showed a maggot emerging from a fruit. This was meant to send a message that life is full of beautiful things, but in the end everything will rot and decay.

A page from *The Book of Hours of Mary of Burgundy* (1480). The artist tried to make the flowers look as realistic as possible.

Impressionist images

In the 19th century, a group of artists known as the **Impressionists** took a new approach to still life. Instead of trying to represent nature exactly, they aimed to give an impression of what they saw. These paintings were much less detailed than the Dutch studies. Instead, the artists concentrated on the shapes and colours of the fruit. Paul Cézanne was a French Post-Impressionist artist who was influenced by the Impressionist style.

He made a series of studies of apples and oranges in which he explored the way that light reflected off the surface of the different fruits.

Vegetable portraits

In the late 16th century, Giuseppe Arcimboldo created a set of portraits entirely made up of carefully painted fruits and vegetables. The meaning behind them is likely to be about man's dependence on nature.

Giuseppe Arcimboldo, *Summer* (1573). This portrait of a smiling man is created from fruits, plants, and vegetables that grow in the summer months. It is part of a series of four "vegetable portraits", each representing a different season.

Islamic patterns

The religion of **Islam** teaches that artists should avoid showing any human or animal forms. This means that Islamic artists concentrate on designs inspired by flowers and plants. From the 7th century CE, Islamic artists and craft workers have produced tiles, vases, and carpets, all featuring beautiful flower and plant designs.

Decorative tiles

In many parts of the Islamic world, mosques and palaces are decorated with **ceramic** tiles, which are usually painted in vivid shades of turquoise and blue. These tiles may form a border of intertwined flowers and leaves, or they may cover an entire wall with a repeated flower design. Sometimes several tiles are combined to form a picture showing a branching shrub or tree.

Iznic designs

Since the 7th century CE, potters in Persia (present-day Iran) have been creating exquisite vases decorated with flowers. However, around the 16th century, a distinctive new style of pottery developed in Turkey. The style was known as "Iznic", and Iznic pots and plates are made today in Turkey, Iran, and Pakistan. They feature delicate branching flowers, which are usually painted in deep blues, turquoises, and greens, against a white background.

Persian carpets

Around 500 CE, weavers in Persia began to create carpet designs based on real gardens. A description of an early royal carpet explains that the carpet was based on the king's garden, and its wide borders showed real flowerbeds, filled with spring flowers. Carpets were made using different colours to show gardens at different times of year. Later these designs developed into more abstract patterns, but the images of flowers remain.

Inlaid marble

The Taj Mahal in northern India was completed in 1643. It was built as a lasting memorial to the wife of Emperor Shah Jahan, and it is one of the world's most magnificent buildings. The Taj was built from white marble and its walls were decorated with patterns made from precious stones, set into the marble. The patterns on the Taj Mahal show delicate leaves and flowers in a range of pale colours. Marble workers in northern India still create flower patterns based on the designs in the Taj Mahal.

Patterns from India

In the 1700s, European traders began to export printed fabric from southern India. This fabric was known as *"chintes"*, and it showed traditional patterns of brightly coloured flowers and birds. The Indian patterns were copied by European manufacturers, who called their fabric "chintz". Today, chintz is still used for curtains and chair covers.

A beautifully decorated mosque in the city of Isfahan, Iran. The striking patterns on the dome are paintings of flowers and leaves.

Chinese flower painting

The art of flower painting started in China in the 10th century CE. It began at the court of the Song emperors and spread rapidly throughout China. Chinese flower painters used two very different styles, and both of these traditions have continued in China.

Some artists created careful paintings that were filled with detail. Painters on porcelain copied this style to create delicate floral patterns on china vases and dishes.

Other flower painters produced much looser and freer images. They painted directly onto paper or silk and tried to give the impression of the flower rather than its details. This style of flower painting is still practiced today in China and Japan. Before an artist starts to paint a flower, he or she studies the flower calmly and tries to understand it. Then the artist paints the flower, using just a few elegant brushstrokes.

Wild flowers

Some artists in the West have recognized the powerful energy of flowers. They have tried to show this energy in their paintings. In the 1880s, the Dutch painter Vincent van Gogh produced several paintings of *Sunflowers*. All these paintings show a simple bunch of sunflowers in a jug. The sunflowers are painted in a range of yellows, oranges, and browns, which all glow brilliantly. They seem to have a powerful inner energy as they twist and turn in different directions.

Some of van Gogh's sunflowers are in bud, some are in full bloom, and some are dying. This makes his paintings look interesting, but also gives a message about the stages of life.

A delicate study of orchids, painted in Japan in the 16th century. The flowers are carefully arranged to create a balanced shape.

Vincent van Gogh, *Sunflowers* (1888). Van Gogh's famous painting is much more than just a study of flowers in a jug. It expresses the golden, sun-filled nature of the flowers, which seem filled with energy as they twist and turn in all directions.

The American artist Georgia O'Keeffe began painting flowers in the early 1900s. Her large-scale paintings usually view a single flower from very close up, as if she was looking at it from an insect's point of view. O'Keeffe concentrates on the structures and colours of plants. She creates paintings that are almost abstract.

While Georgia O'Keeffe was working in America, another woman artist, Margaret Preston, was painting the plants of Australia. Preston was strongly influenced by Australian Aboriginal art. She used dramatic black outlines to emphasize the Australian plants' strange and spiky shapes.

35

Horses, dogs, and cattle

As soon as people started hunting and farming, they had an important connection to animals. In the Stone Age, hunting images were painted on cave walls. Models of working animals have survived from the earliest civilizations.

Model animals

People started farming in India around 3500 BCE The Indus Valley farmers used oxen to plough their fields, and artists produced clay models of oxen. One surviving model has a nodding head. Similar figures of working animals survive from Ancient Egypt. **Archaeologists** believe that some of these models were placed in tombs, to accompany farmers to the next world. However, some of the models have moving parts, and these were probably children's toys.

Sculptures of horses

The sculptors of Ancient Greece and Rome concentrated on scenes from history or tales of the gods. These scenes often featured splendid horses, either riding in processions or in the heat of battle. The horses would be carefullly measured, but some features could be exaggerated to make them look more powerful. These striking sculptures show an understanding of real horses.

Around 180 CE a remarkable bronze sculpture was set up in Rome. It shows the emperor Marcus Aurelius seated on his horse. This is believed to be one of the world's finest **equestrian monuments**. It looks equally realistic from all angles.

This bronze statue of the Roman emperor Marcus Aurelius on his horse was made almost 2,000 years ago. The horse is remarkably realistic.

Horses of the Renaissance

After the collapse of the Roman Empire, the skills of many artists were lost. Images of horses from the Middle Ages often look flat and clumsy. However, things began to change in the 15th century when the Italian **Renaissance** began (see panel). The sculptor Donatello created a strikingly realistic sculpture of the Italian soldier Gattamelata mounted on his horse. Meanwhile, Leonardo da Vinci made a series of careful studies of horses and other animals, concentrating on the way the muscles and tendons worked under the skin. Gradually, artists all over Europe began to show horses and other animals in a much more life-like way.

The Italian Renaissance

Around 1400, Italian artists began to rediscover the lost artwork of the Greeks and Romans. Instead of just copying these pieces, 15th-century artists improved on them. The new style of painting and sculpture spread gradually north, throughout Europe. This period is known as the "Renaissance", which means "rebirth" in Italian.

Paolo Uccello, *Monument to Sir John Hawkwood* (1436). Renaissance artists became very interested in painting horses. In this painting of a great soldier, the horse seems almost more important than its rider.

37

Racehorses

By 1800, horse racing was very popular, and artists would have been **commissioned** to paint horses. One of the most famous artists of race horses was George Stubbs. He usually painted horses away from the racecourse, preferring to spend time in their stables, studying their individual characters. Stubbs learned about the **anatomy** of horses by **dissecting** the bodies of dead horses, so that he could understand exactly how their muscles worked.

Photographing horses

Paintings and prints showing horses racing were very fashionable in the 19th century. These images showed horses galloping full-tilt across the countryside, with two legs stretched out in front and two behind. However, some people claimed that this was not the way that real horses galloped.

In the 1870s, the photographer Eadweard Muybridge settled this question forever by taking a series of still photographs of a horse in motion. His experiment involved placing 24 cameras at intervals along a track. He then made a projector which could show all these images in sequence. Muybridge showed that when horses gallop, each foot touches the ground in turn. His experiments marked the start of moving photography.

Eadweard Muybridge, *Man and Horse Jumping a Fence* (1887). Muybridge created many photo sequences of horses in motion. His work changed the way that artists showed horses.

Wild horses

The German painter Franz Marc was one of the founders of the Expressionist movement. The **Expressionists** painted in a bold, confident style, using vivid colours, and their paintings were full of feeling and emotion. Many of the Expressionists painted scenes with people, but Marc concentrated mainly on horses. Marc's dream-like images of wild horses give a sense of the mysterious power of the animal world. His groups of prancing horses appear to be performing a secret dance.

The Italian sculptor Marino Marini produced a series of bronze sculptures showing small human figures perched on the backs of massive horses.

In one of these works, *Horse and Rider*, the horse strains upwards and forwards while its tiny rider is thrown backwards. The rider seems unable to control the energy and power of his horse.

Scythian horses

The Scythian people lived on the Russian plains around 700 BCE. They spent most of their lives on horseback, but also created simple iron sculptures and pictures made from felt. Some Scythian sculptures and pictures show horses in motion. These ancient images seem remarkably modern in their sense of the power and speed of the wild horses.

Franz Marc, *Little Blue Horse* (1912). Marc was fascinated by wild horses. His colourful horses in their fantasy landscape have a magical, fairy-tale quality.

Prize possessions

In the 18th century, artists often painted farm animals to show off their excellent size and condition. Rich farmers and landowners paid artists to produce portraits of enormous bulls, sheep, and pigs, standing proudly against a country landscape. In these **formal** portraits, the animals are often shown standing obediently beside their masters.

Animals in the landscape

By the 19th century, artists were creating more romantic images of animals in the countryside. The English painter John Constable produced idealised scenes of cows grazing and horses pulling hay wagons. Constable spent a lot of time outdoors, sketching real scenes with oil paints. He then used these sketches to produce large, imaginary scenes in his studio. Meanwhile, Sir Edwin Landseer painted large studies of cattle or deer standing proudly against the wild Scottish landscape.

Pet dogs

People have kept dogs as pets since Roman times. A mosaic found in the Roman town of Pompeii pictures a lively looking black dog on a red lead. A 15th-century portrait of Saint Augustine shows the saint in his study with a small pet dog. In 1542, the great Italian artist Titian painted a portrait of the two-year-old Clarissa Strozzi with her pet spaniel. The young girl has her arms around the dog, who is sitting on a table.

The 18th-century portrait painter Thomas Gainsborough often included pet dogs in his portraits. In many of these paintings, pet dogs are shown leaping up to be fondled, or even being held in their owner's arms. The dogs in Gainsborough's portraits vary from beautifully groomed long-haired collies to sad-looking mongrels. One of his most appealing paintings shows a ragged "cottage girl" clutching a puppy in her arms, while they both stare sadly out of the portrait.

In 1842, a proud landowner paid an artist to record the massive size of his prize-winning cow. In the background of the picture is the landowner's home.

Dogs with character

In the 20th century, two very different sculptors produced amusing images of dogs. In 1951, the Swiss sculptor Alberto Giacometti created a spindly, bronze sculpture simply entitled *Dog*. It shows a skinny, long-legged hound, with floppy ears, lolloping along with its nose pointed down.

In 1992, the American artist Jeff Koons came up with the idea for a giant floral sculpture. It is called *Puppy* and it is made up entirely of flowers grown over a frame. Koon's sculpture forms the instantly recognizable outline of a seated "Westie" terrier. It emphasizes the cute and toy-like nature of the pet dog.

Jeff Koons, *Puppy* (1992-). Koons' sculpture was first shown in Germany, and has since been to galleries all over the world. Koons describes it as a symbol of "love, warmth and happiness".

Cats, birds, and fish

Pet cats

After the Ancient Egyptian period, very few domestic cats featured in paintings or sculpture. However, in the 19th century, pet cats began to appear once more in art. In particular, several portrait painters showed cats with their owners.

The American painter Mary Cassatt worked at the turn of the 19th and 20th centuries and painted several portraits of children with their cats. In the painting *Sara Holding a Cat*, a young girl holds her ginger cat protectively, concentrating all her attention on her pet. Another Mary Cassatt painting shows two children playing with a cat. A little girl holds a pet cat on her knee while her baby brother stretches out to stroke it. In these two charming paintings, cats are shown as soft and gentle creatures.

Black cat

At around the same time as Mary Cassatt was painting her pictures of cats, the French poster designer Théophile Steinlen was producing a very different image. Steinlen's famous *Chat Noir* poster was designed in the bold **Art Nouveau** style and advertised the Black Cat nightclub in Paris. The design is dominated by the striking figure of a seated cat, staring straight out of the poster. The cat is entirely black, apart from a pair of large yellow eyes. Steinlen makes his cat seem extra wild and menacing by adding sprouting eyebrows and whiskers.

In 1939, the famous Spanish artist Pablo Picasso revealed the savage side of the domestic cat in his painting *Cat Seizing a Bird*. This dramatic work shows a pet cat in the act of catching a bird. Picasso uses a simple, flat style, rather like a child's drawing. At first sight, this may seem like a harmless picture, but Picasso has created a frightening image of the cat's cruel and savage nature.

Wild cats

Artists have always been inspired by wild cats. In many parts of China, people wear lion masks and perform elaborate lion dances in the street (see picture on page 5). These traditional costumes and dances have remained unchanged for hundreds of years. In Ancient China, people believed that if they took on the appearance of a lion, they would gain some of that creature's strength and power.

Some artists have tried to show the ferocity of tigers and other wild cats. The 19th-century artist and poet William Blake wrote a famous poem about a tiger and illustrated it himself. Blake's poem begins with the powerful lines, "Tyger, Tyger, burning bright, In the forests of the night: ..."

In the 1890s, Henri Rousseau produced a series of dramatic paintings showing tigers pouncing on their prey (see page 4). In 1912, Franz Marc painted *The Tiger*.

In this powerful painting, the tiger slinks across the picture, and turns to look over its shoulder with a cool stare.

Pablo Picasso, *Cat Seizing a Bird* (1939). Picasso's image of a domestic cat is deliberately shocking. It provides a frightening reminder of a tiger attacking its prey.

Ancient birds

Birds have featured in art for thousands of years. Artists in Ancient Egypt painted **realistic** images of geese and other water birds, while the Chinese tradition of painting birds began in the 10th century CE.

Birds of China

In China, there are two main methods of painting birds. One method involves careful observation, drawing, and painting of details. This type of bird painting is also used on china plates and bowls. The other method of painting birds is more sketchy, as the artist paints directly onto the paper, using coloured inks. These lively bird paintings express the playful nature of birds.

Hokusai and Audubon

By the 18th century, the Chinese art of bird painting had spread to Japan. One of the most original Japanese bird artists was the print-maker Hokusai. He created many colourful woodblock prints featuring birds. Hokusai's most famous bird print is *Flock of Chickens*. Using only three basic colours — red, white, and black — Hokusai shows seven roosters nestling closely together against a pale blue background, creating a circle of motion with their swirling feathers.

While Hokusai was designing his dramatic prints, an American artist was producing very different images of birds.

John James Audubon worked in the tradition of careful, scientific observation of birds. He created hundreds of detailed bird studies in America and Great Britain.

Hokusai, *Azaleas and Cuckoo*. This simple but dramatic print shows the free spirit of the cuckoo as it swoops and dives above the brilliant flowers.

Abstract birds

Some modern sculptors have produced **semi-abstract** images of birds. These adventurous works of art do not show recognizable birds. Instead they use forms and shapes to express the character of birds.

During the first half of the 20th century, the American artist Alexander Calder created a series of bird sculptures. *Hen* is made from pieces of polished wood, arranged in a shape that looks like a hen. *Flamingo* is a giant metal structure painted bright scarlet. *Big Bird* is made from two pieces of metal shaped to give an impression of wings, a beak, and a tail.

Calder also produced a series of mobiles that explore the nature of flight. Some of the shapes used look like feathers or wings. Others look like flying birds.

David Smith's *Big Rooster* (1945) is made from scrap metal. It looks like a cross between a bird and a machine, but a beak, a comb, and feathers can be recognized.

Alexander Calder, *Big Bird* (1937). Many of Calder's sculptures resemble cartoon drawings. In this simple structure Calder has used a few basic shapes to create the impression of a cheeky bird.

Images of fish

Around the 8th century CE, some Chinese monks began to keep carp in ponds. Carp are red-and-orange coloured fish, rather like goldfish. By the time of the **Ming dynasty**, in the 14th century CE, Chinese artists were painting images of carp on porcelain and silk. They also carved sculptures of carp out of jade. At first, the artists painted the fish from above, but when people started using glass-sided fish tanks, artists began to show side views of fish.

A special symbol

In ancient China, the carp was a symbol of courage. It was said that the carp could jump over the rapids of the Yellow River, leaving all the other fish behind. Today, Chinese scholars use the carp as a good luck symbol, to help them gain higher scores in their exams. In Chinese art, two fish swimming together are seen as a symbol of harmony and married bliss. Traditional Chinese wedding gifts are often decorated with pictures of fish.

A selection of Chinese porcelain. Swimming carp often feature on Chinese dishes and vases. Some are realistic images of fish, but other carp designs are more stylized and decorative.

Paintings and porcelain

Ever since the 14th century, Chinese artists have been creating colourful paintings on silk, showing carp weaving their way through water lilies, rocks, and weeds. In these delicate paintings, the graceful, scarlet fish stand out boldly against a pale blue, watery background. Recently, some Chinese artists have concentrated on the patterns made by the swimming fish, and created almost abstract works.

Carp designs on Chinese porcelain have developed in two very different directions. Some porcelain vases, plates, and bowls feature detailed and decorative images of fish. However, the Chinese have also created a simplified carp design. This bold design shows a simple fish shape, which is painted in vivid blue against a plain white background. Chinese blue-and-white porcelain, featuring the carp design, has become popular throughout the world.

Matisse's goldfish

In 1912, the famous French artist Henri Matisse painted *Goldfish*. This painting shows a tank of goldfish standing on a table surrounded by flowers. Goldfish were an important symbol for Matisse, and he painted several pictures of them. Matisse explained that he saw the fish as representing colour, life, and movement. He liked to watch them swimming calmly and silently. He found that the goldfish helped him to feel peaceful and thoughtful.

Henri Matisse, *Goldfish* (1911). Matisse was strongly influenced by oriental art. His paintings of goldfish combine plants and fish to create a picture that is filled with pattern – rather like the designs on Chinese vases and plates.

47

Exotic creatures

People have always been fascinated by unusual animals. Before the age of the camera, artists produced images of creatures from far-off lands for people to marvel at. Sometimes these pictures were based on real animals, but often the artists had never seen the creatures they showed.

Elephants and whales

During the Middle Ages, artists attempted to draw creatures from distant countries that they had never visited. They based their pictures on travellers' tales, which were often inaccurate or wrong. Artists also copied each other's images, and reproduced the same mistakes again and again.

Medieval manuscripts feature some very interesting images of elephants.

Some have very long legs and horses' hooves and tails. Many have tiny ears or no ears at all, and some have trunks shaped like trumpets. Medieval images of whales are equally surprising. Some are covered in scales and look like enormous fish, while others have large snouts and pointed fangs.

Portraits of rhinos

In 1515, the German artist Albrecht Dürer created a detailed picture of a rhinoceros, even though he had never seen one. Dürer's famous picture was based on a sketch and description sent to him by a friend. It shows the rhinoceros, encased in plates of thick hide, rather like a suit of armour. However, in spite of its errors, Dürer's rhinoceros became famous throughout Europe.

Albrecht Dürer, *Rhinoceros* (1515). Dürer's rhinoceros is a strange-looking beast with a second horn on its back. But it is certainly a brilliant work of art.

It was copied many times — carved on doors, painted on china, and even made into a bronze statue.

Another image of a rhinoceros was painted by Pietro Longhi in 1751. This painting shows the rhinoceros on display in Venice. It has had its horn removed and looks very dejected. Meanwhile, an audience of masked ladies and gentleman has come to stare. Longhi's painting leaves a sad impression. It shows how a noble animal can be turned into a public show. People are still concerned that some animals are treated like this in zoos and circuses today.

An elegant giraffe

In 1841, Jacques-Laurent Agasse painted *The Nubian Giraffe*. This painting shows the tall and graceful creature with its keepers in an English country setting. During the 19th century, wealthy landowners in Europe often imported exotic animals, and artists were paid to paint these creatures. Agasse's painting was paid for by George IV. It is a very skilful work of art, but the viewer is left with the question: Why has this beautiful, gentle creature been forced to travel to such a strange new land?

Pietro Longhi, *Exhibition of a Rhinoceros in Venice* (1751). The man on the left is holding the rhino's horn and a whip. Is this painting a protest against cruelty to animals?

Animal stories and characters

For thousands of years, people have told stories about animals. One of the oldest sets of animal tales is *Aesop's Fables*. These famous stories were told in Ancient Egypt and were written down in Ancient Greece. The animals in *Aesop's Fables* stand for different kinds of human beings, and every story teaches a lesson. The *Fables* include the story of the race between the tortoise and the hare, which has been illustrated hundreds of times.

Legends around the world

Each civilization has its own animal legends, and many of these stories have lessons to teach. One set of stories from the Caribbean tells the adventures of Ananse the spider. Ananse is small and weak but also very clever. He always manages to trick the larger animals just by using his brain. The moral of the Ananse stories is that the "little person" can often be right in the end.

Stories and films

The tradition of telling animal stories has continued right up to the present day. Rudyard Kipling's *The Jungle Book*, about the adventures of a boy called Mowgli and his animal friends, was published in 1894. Kenneth Graham's *The Wind in the Willows*, telling the adventures of Rat, Mole, and Toad, was published in 1908. In 1952, E. B. White wrote *Charlotte's Web*, the story of a spider and a pig.

All these animal stories became children's classics, which are still read today.

By the 1940s, animal stories were appearing on the big screen, usually in the form of cartoons. One of the first animal cartoon films was *Bambi*, the story of a baby deer, which was produced by Walt Disney in 1942. More than sixty years on, Disney studios are still producing animal films such as *The Lion King* and *Finding Nemo*.

Animal characters

Some animal characters from stories and films have become world famous. Some Disney animal characters, such as Mickey Mouse and Donald Duck, can be instantly recognized, and artists have even used some of these famous characters in their work. The Swedish-born U.S. **sculptor** Claes Oldenburg has created a series of sculptures called *Geometric Mouse*. The sculptures are made from simple **geometric** shapes that are linked together to form the famous outline of the head of Mickey Mouse.

Animal appeal

Animals have always fascinated artists. From the paintings of bison made in prehistoric times, to the cartoon images of the 21st century, artists have tried to capture the spirit of their fellow creatures in the living world.

Gaston Gelibert, *The Young Cockerel, the Cat and the Young Mouse*, from *Fables by Jean de la Fontaine* (1888). Jean de la Fontaine was a 17th-century French poet who wrote a famous collection of animal stories with morals. His fables have been illustrated many times and are still read today.

Map and Further reading

NORWAY
GERMANY
HOLLAND
UNITED
KINGDOM
EUROPE
RUSSIA
ASIA
FRANCE
ITALY
SPAIN
GREECE
CHINA
JAPAN
UNITED STATES
OF AMERICA
Atlantic Ocean
EGYPT
SAUDI
ARABIA
Pacific Ocean
MEXICO
AFRICA
Pacific Ocean
BRAZIL
Indian Ocean
PERU
AUSTRALIA

Map of the world

This map shows you roughly where in the world some key works of art discussed in this book were produced. The countries marked on the map relate to entries in the timeline, opposite.

Further Reading

History in Art series
(Raintree, 2005)

Directions in Art series
(Heinemann Library, 2003)

Art in History series
(Heinemann Library, 2001)

Eyewitness Art: Looking at Paintings, Jude Welton, (Dorling Kindersley, 1994)

Timeline

This timeline provides approximate dates of some key works of art. The entries are linked to countries marked on the map of the world, opposite.

BCE

c.30,000 People in Europe make cave paintings of wild animals

c.20,000 Aboriginal people in Australia begin to create images of animal Spirit Ancestors

Africans paint animals on rock walls

c.1400 The ancient Egyptians create images of animal gods. They also show cats and hippos in their art.

c.700 The Scythians show horses in motion (central Asia)

c.500 The Ancient Chinese begin to show dragons in their art

c.400 Ancient Greek sculptors create realistic images of horses and lions

c.300 Native American hunters wear animal costumes for hunting. They also carve totem poles decorated with animal heads.

c.200 Mayan people carve stone jaguar heads (modern-day Mexico)

CE

c.400 Nazca potters make jars shaped like animals (Peru)

c.500 Hindus in India begin to carve statues of their animal gods

c.700 Islamic artists begin to create flower and plant designs for tiles, vases, and carpets.

c.800 The Vikings carve dragon heads on the prows of their ships (Norway)

c.1000 Flower painting begins in China

c.1200 Medieval artists in Europe begin to show detailed plants and flowers in manuscripts, carvings, and tapestries. They also show mythical beasts.

c.1300 Artists in China begin creating fish designs

c.1400 Artists of the Italian Renaissance create realistic images of animals

c.1600 Painters in the Netherlands produce realistic studies of flowers and fruit

c.1700 Artists begin to produce detailed botanical drawings of plants

1770s George Stubbs paints horses (UK)

1830s Hokusai produces prints of birds (Japan)

1850s Sir Edwin Landseer paints animals in the landscape (UK)

1880s Vincent van Gogh produces his sunflower paintings (Holland)

Eadweard Muybridge photographs running horses (UK)

1890s Henry Rousseau paints pictures of tigers (France)

1912 Henri Matisse paints *Goldfish* (France)

Franz Marc paints *Little Blue Horse* (Germany)

1937 Alexander Calder makes his sculpture *Big Bird* (USA)

1939 Pablo Picasso paints *Cat Seizing a Bird* (Spain)

1992 Jeff Koons creates his sculpture *Puppy* (USA)

Glossary

Aboriginal people people who have lived in a country for thousands of years, before later settlers arrived

abstract showing an idea rather than a thing

acanthus a plant with stiff, pointed leaves

anatomy the structure of a human or animal body

ancestor a family member who lived a long time ago

anonymous produced by someone whose name is not known

archaeologist someone who studies the past by uncovering old objects or buildings and examining them carefully

Art Nouveau a style in art and architecture which used swirling shapes and patterns, based on forms found in nature. Art Nouveau began in France in the 1890s.

bark painting a painting made on a piece of flattened tree bark

bestiary a type of illustrated manuscript from the Middle Ages

botany the study of plants

ceramic made from fired clay

charcoal black substance made by burning wood

clan a group of people who share the same ancestors and customs

coat-of-arms a design in the shape of a shield that is used as the special sign of a family

codex/codices handmade book/s

commission to pay an artist to create a work of art

constellation a group of stars that forms a shape or pattern

dissect to cut up a body or another structure, in order to learn more about it

eland a type of antelope

equestrian monument a statue of a man seated on a horse

etch to carve a design into a hard surface such as metal or glass

Expressionist a style in art which aims to express the artist's emotions and which uses bold shapes and colours

formal stiff, well-behaved, and not casual

geometric using forms found in geometry, such as a square, a triangle and a circle

Hindu a follower of Hinduism, the main religion and culture of India and Nepal

Impressionist a style of art in which artists try to show the impression that something has on their senses

incarnation the form that a person or a god can take

Islam religion and way of life followed by Muslims

jade a green stone that can be easily carved

knight a man who fought on horseback in the Middle Ages

manuscript a hand-written book

medieval belonging to the period from approximately 1000 CE to 1450 CE

medium/media a method used by an artist. Drawing, painting and sculpture, are all different media.

Middle Ages the period of history between approximately 1000 CE and 1450 CE

Ming dynasty the period in Chinese history when the country was ruled by members of the Ming family. The Ming dynasty lasted from 1368 CE to 1644 CE.

Mosaic a picture or pattern made up of tiny pieces of coloured stone or glass

mummy a dead body that has been preserved in special liquids and wrapped in cloth so that it will last for a very long time

mythical connected to an ancient story or legend

pharoah an Ancient Egyptian ruler

pigment paint made from natural materials such as earth

porcelain fine china

portray to show something or someone through art, music or writing

prehistoric belonging to a time millions of years ago, before history was written down

prow the pointed front of a ship

psalter prayer book

realistic very like the real thing

Renaissance a movement in art and learning that took place in Europe between the 14th and 16th centuries. Renaissance artists aimed to produce more realistic works of art than before, and were partly inspired by the art of the Ancient Greeks and Romans.

sacred holy

sculptor someone who makes works of art from stone, wood, metal or other materials

sculpture a work of art made from stone, wood, metal or other materials

semi-abstract style of art that concentrates on ideas rather than things, but whose subject can still be recognized

semi-precious stones rocks or gems, such as jade, that look beautiful but are not as expensive as precious stones, such as diamonds

still life a painting or drawing showing objects that are not alive

tapestry a heavy piece of cloth with pictures or patterns woven into it

textiles fabrics or materials

totem pole a carved and painted pole made by Native Americans. Totem poles have special religious meanings.

Index

Titles in the *Through Artists' Eyes* series include:

Hardback   1 406 20151 0

Hardback   1 406 20153 7

Hardback   1 406 20152 9

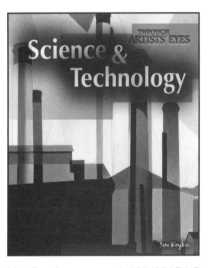

Hardback   1 406 20154 5

Hardback   1 406 20150 2

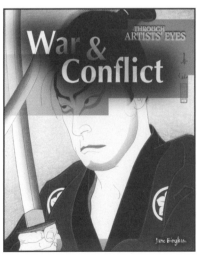

Hardback   1 406 20149 9

Find out about other raintree titles on our website www.raintreelibrary.co.uk